I Can Draw
FOREST
Animals

Please visit our web site at: www.garethstevens.com
For a free color catalog describing Gareth Stevens' list of high-quality books and multimedia programs, call 1-800-542-2595 (USA) or 1-800-461-9120 (Canada). Gareth Stevens Publishing's Fax: (414) 332-3567.

Library of Congress Cataloging-in-Publication Data

Leroux-Hugon, Hélène.
    [Animaux de la forêt. English]
    I can draw forest animals / by Hélène Leroux-Hugon.
        p. cm. — (I can draw animals!)
    Includes bibliographical references and index.
    ISBN 0-8368-2839-9 (lib. bdg.)
    1. Forest animals in art—Juvenile literature.   2. Drawing—Technique—Juvenile literature. [1. Forest animals in art.   2. Drawing—Technique.] I. Title.
NC783.8.F67L4713   2001
743.6'9—dc21   00-053148

This edition first published in 2001 by
Gareth Stevens Publishing
A World Almanac Education Group Company
330 West Olive Street, Suite 100
Milwaukee, Wisconsin 53212 USA

This U.S. edition © 2001 by Gareth Stevens, Inc. Original edition first published by Larousse-Bordas, Paris, France, under the title *Les animaux de la Forêt*, © Dessain et Tolra/HER 2000. Additional end matter © 2001 by Gareth Stevens, Inc.

Illustrations: Hélène Leroux-Hugon
Photography: Cactus Studio
Translation: Valerie J. Weber
English text: Valerie J. Weber
Gareth Stevens editor: Katherine Meitner
Cover design: Katherine Kroll

Printed in the United States of America

  2 3 4 5 6 7 8 9 05 04 03 02

I Can Draw
FOREST
Animals

Hélène Leroux-Hugon

Gareth Stevens Publishing
A WORLD ALMANAC EDUCATION GROUP COMPANY

Table of Contents

I Can Draw

Observing

Without pencil or paper, take a walk in the forest and watch the animals. If you can't go to the woods, find books about forest animals with pictures. These will help you see animals in a different way.

Try to find simple geometric forms, such as circles or ovals, in these animals.

Practicing

Without using a stencil or a compass, draw circles, ovals, and curves by hand. This is called freestyle drawing. Notice that your circle may not be perfectly round and that an oval can be wide or narrow, short or long.

Drawing by Steps

Now choose your model in this book — for example, the fox.

1 The fox is made up of an oval for the body, a circle for the head, and two lines for the neck (see page 16). Step by step, draw the form with a light mark. At the beginning, of course, your drawing is simple. This stage is called a sketch; it helps you see the size of the head compared to the size of the body and exactly where each body part goes.

6

2 Add details such as the fox's ears and muzzle. Begin the paws and the tail. Don't press too hard on your pencil because you're going to make several marks on the paper before deciding which one is the best. You will have to erase the marks shown as dotted lines on the model.

3 Draw the eyes, the inside of the ears, and the whiskers. Finish the paws and the beautiful, furry tail. Look at the model and redraw the outline to make the lines smoother and more lifelike. And there, your drawing is finished!

Now you're free to color and to complete some big drawings where you'll put several different animals in their natural environment.

While you are drawing, you will also learn many things about animals and their habitats. Look for the footprint left by the animal at the bottom of the page. Here, it's the fox.

Sometimes the animal doesn't have a footprint, and in this case, you will find a tiny drawing of the animal at the bottom of the page. Here, it's the stag beetle.

7

The Doe and the Fawn

1 Draw a large oval for the body, a little one for the head, and two lines for the neck.

2 Reshape the head and add two ears and a muzzle. Begin the tail and the legs. Erase your marks at the dotted line.

3 Draw the inside of the ears, tail, and finish the hooves. Don't forget the little eye and the round tummy!

Deer eat tree leaves and bark, grasses, and many other green plants. The male deer is called a buck and lives alone. The female deer is called a doe and lives in herds in the forest. At the end of spring, she gives birth to a small, spotted fawn.

The Boar Family

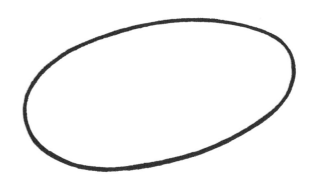

1 Trace a big oval for the boar's body. Notice how the oval slants.

2 Add the ears, the muzzle, and the tail, and sketch in the legs. The dotted lines show which marks to erase.

3 Finish the ears, the hooves, and the snout. Draw the eye. Look at the shape of your boar and then the example shown here. See if you can make your drawing even better!

At night or even at dawn, the boar digs in the forest ground with its snout, looking for chestnuts, roots, and worms.

In spring, the female boar, called the sow, gives birth to young wild boars called piglets. Piglets have brown-and-yellow striped fur.

The Colorful Pheasant

1 Draw a big oval for the pheasant's body and put a little circle on top for its head.

2 Add the beak, the wing, and the tail. Fill out the stomach and draw the legs. Erase the dotted lines.

3 Draw its eye and the crest on top of its head, then finish the tail and the feet. Look at the pretty feathers and necklace around its neck. Isn't the pheasant beautiful?

Pheasants live in the woods and prairies, where they eat seeds and fruits. The male pheasant has colorful feathers that are magnificent. The female pheasant has brown spotted feathers that help her hide from predators.

In the Clearing

The forest is full of many kinds of trees and plants, including mushrooms, ferns and mosses. Different kinds of trees and plants grow in different forests depending on the climate and the soil.

The trees shown here are deciduous trees. They have leaves that change color in autumn and fall off in winter.

Animals can find all sorts of shelters and nesting places in the forest, from under the ground to the tops of the trees.

Sly as a Fox

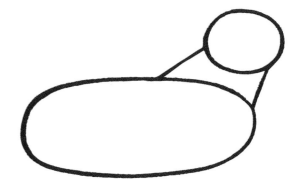

1 Draw a big oval for the body and a circle for the head. Draw two lines for the neck.

2 Add the ears and muzzle. Now begin to sketch the legs and the tail. Then erase the dotted lines.

3 Finish with the paws and the beautiful, fluffy tail. Draw the eyes, the inside of the ears, and the whiskers. Try to improve the whole drawing.

The fox lives in the flat, open countryside, in the forest, and sometimes even near cities. We recognize it by its beautiful red fur. The female gives birth to three to seven babies, called pups, in each litter. The fox chases small prey to eat.

17

Digging Badgers

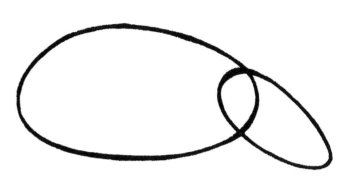

1 Sketch two ovals — a big one for the body and a little one for the head. Notice how the oval for the head slants.

2 Add the ears and the paws. The dotted lines show where you should erase.

3 Draw the eye, muzzle, whiskers, and claws. Add the funny mask. Doesn't he look sneaky?

18

Thanks to the badger's short, powerful paws and sharp claws, it can dig long tunnels under the ground. It lives with its family in a burrow, and it comes out at night to eat. While a badger can eat anything, it especially loves worms, slugs, and snails!

19

The Burrow

Many animals live in a burrow. It is their shelter from the weather and a hiding place from predators. Foxes, badgers, rabbits, and moles all live in burrows.

The badger is the only one of these animals that builds long burrows made of tunnels and rooms that are linked together. Several families live in the burrow. These families may include grandparents, parents, and babies. The badger makes its burrow more comfortable by putting down a layer of leaves and grass.

The Spiny Hedgehog

1 Draw a big oval for the body and a little oval with a pointed end for the head.

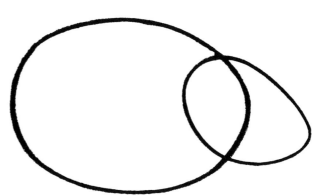

2 Now, draw the muzzle, ears, and paws. Erase the dotted lines.

3 Finish by drawing the eye, whiskers, claws, and the hedgehog's spines. What a funny ball!

The hedgehog lives just as well in the forest as in the fields, the countryside, or the cities. It goes out at night to eat insects, slugs, and worms. When it is frightened, the hedgehog rolls itself up into a ball. Its thousands of spines protect it.

23

Spectacled Dormouse

1 Draw a large oval for the body and a circle for the head.

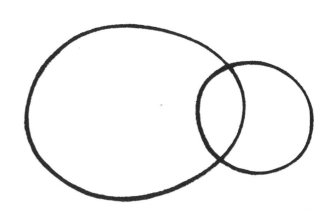

2 Add the ears, paws, and the beginning of the tail. Erase the dotted lines.

3 Next, add the eyes, muzzle, whiskers, and tail. Doesn't it look mischievous?

You can recognize a dormouse by its black mask. Most dormice also have bushy tails. The dormouse is a rodent that eats nuts and fruit like apples, but it especially likes insects. It lives in rocky and stony areas and makes its nest in tree hollows.

Croak! Croak! A Toad

1 Draw an oval for the toad's body. It looks like an egg!

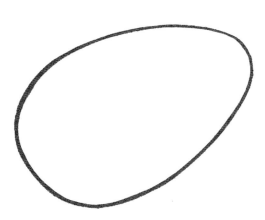

2 Sketch the short front legs and the strong back legs. The dotted lines show which lines you can erase.

3 Add the eye and the warts on its back. Try to improve the outline. Look out, it's going to jump!

The skin of the toad is covered with warts. Most toads are shy. They live in holes that are under stones, leaving at night to eat insects. In winter, toads hide in the ground. The female lays many thousands of eggs, from which tadpoles will emerge.

On the Ground

The forest ground is home to many different kinds of animals. Every animal can find the right hiding, nesting, or sleeping place.

The hedgehog, for example, lives above the ground. To hibernate or to raise babies, hedgehogs build nests of dry leaves under thick bushes.

Can you find the beautiful animal with a coat all marbled in yellow in this picture? It's a salamander, and it's related to the toad.

The Musical Woodpecker

1 Draw a circle for the head and an oval for the body.

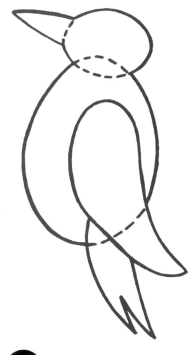

2 Add the beak, wing, and tail. Erase the dotted lines.

3 Finish drawing the beak. Add the eye, feet, feather design, and tree where it stands.

The woodpecker lives where there are trees, from rain forests to city parks. Its sharp claws help it cling to trees. When it needs food, the woodpecker drums its beak on the tree to attract the insects that live in the wood.

The Wild Marten

1 Draw a small circle for the head, a big one for the thighs, and two curving lines for the body.

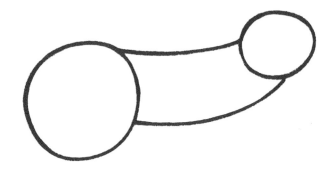

2 Sketch the muzzle, ears, paws, and tail. The dotted lines show which marks you should erase.

3 Look at the model and finish the ears, the paws, and the tail. Add the eyes, the long nose, the whiskers, and the chest.

With its sharp claws, the graceful marten can easily climb among the tree branches. It finds shelter in tree hollows or in old nests, which it lines with moss and dry grasses. The marten eats rodents, insects, birds, and birds' eggs.

33

The Stag Beetle

1 Sketch a circle for the
head, an oval for the body, and
two curving lines for the middle.

2 Add the mandibles
(pinchers) and the legs.
Erase the dotted lines.

3 Finish your drawing by
adding the antennae, the
eyes, and the patterns on
the carapace.

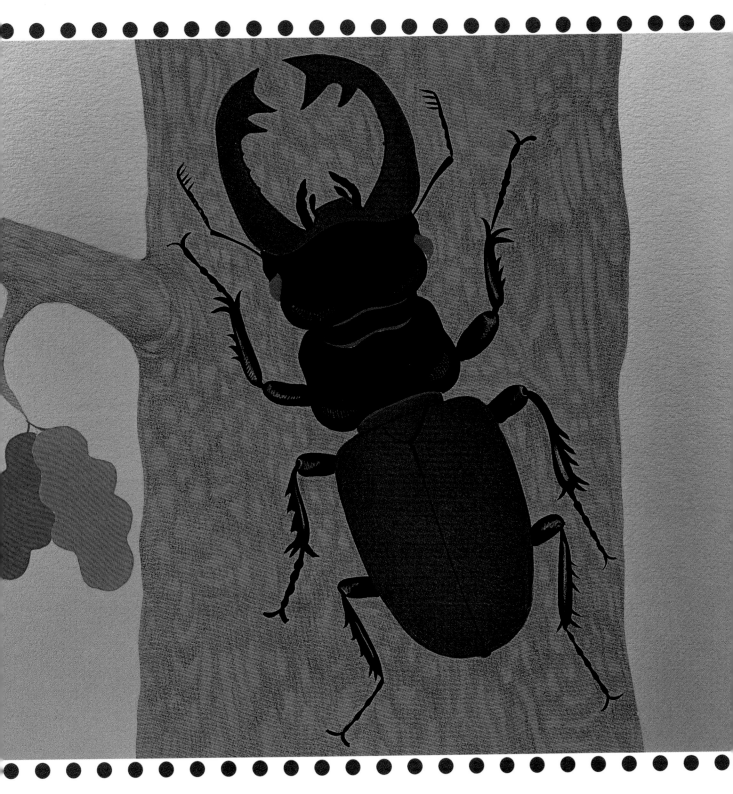

We call this insect a stag beetle because its mandibles look a little like the antlers of a male deer, sometimes called a stag.

The male uses its mandibles to fight other male stag beetles. Stag beetles can grow to nearly 2 inches (5 centimeters) long.

In the Tree

An entire world of animals can live in a tree, even though some of its residents never meet each other. Birds, of course, nest there, and other animals, like the marten or the squirrel, live in the trees and sometimes come down to the ground.

Some animals live in the stumps of dead trees where the wood is rotting. Many insects eat this soft wood and dig out nests where their larvae can grow.

More to Read and View

Books about Drawing

I Can Draw That!: Easy Animals and Monsters (Books and Stuff). Robert Pierce (Grosset & Dunlap)

I Can Draw That, Too!: People, Places, and Things (Books and Stuff). Robert Pierce (Grosset & Dunlap)

Kids Can Draw Animals (Kids Can Draw). Philippe Legendre (Walter Foster)

Learn to Draw for Ages Six and Up. Nina Kidd (Lowell House)

Mark Kistler's Draw Squad. Mark Kistler (Fireside)

Mark Kistler's Imagination Station/Learn How to Draw in 3-D with Public Television's Favorite Drawing Teacher. Mark Kistler (Fireside)

Videos

Doodle: Drawing Animals (A & F Video)

Dan Mahuta: Drawing Made Easy (A & F Video)

Web Sites

Learn to Draw with Billy Bear: www.billybear4kids.com

Draw & Color with Uncle Fred: www.unclefred.com

Some web sites stay current longer than others. To find additional web sites, enter key words based on animals and habitats you've read about in this book, such as *drawing, deer, badger, dormouse, woodpecker, beetle, toad, burrow,* and *forest.*

Glossary/Index

You can find these words on the pages listed.

boar — a wild pig or hog with a hairy coat and long snout 10, 11

burrow — a hole or empty space that is dug into the ground, providing a home to foxes, badgers, rabbits, and other animals 19, 21

carapace — a bony or horny shield covering the back or part of the back of an animal. Beetles and some other insects have carapaces, and the shell of a turtle or crab is a carapace 34

compass — a tool that helps draw circles. A compass has two arms — one placed at the center of the circle and another that holds a pencil 6

deciduous — trees with leaves that fall at the end of their growing season 15

descend — to come down; to move from a higher place to a lower one 37

doe — a female deer 9

fawn — a baby deer 9

habitat — the place where an animal or plant lives or grows 7

hibernate — to spend winter in a state like sleep 29

hollow — a hole or empty space inside a tree. Animals build nests in tree hollows 33

hooves — the thick, protective horn-like covering on certain animal feet. Deer, cows, horses, and pigs have hooves 10

larva — the stage of an insect's life after it leaves the egg and before it becomes an adult. An insect larva often looks like a worm 37

litter — baby animals all born at one time from one mother 17

mandible — a mouthpart of certain insects that is used to seize and bite food 34

moss — small, green plants that prefer to live in damp places. Moss does not produce flowers 15, 33

muzzle — part of an animal's head, including its nose, mouth, and jaws 7, 8, 16, 18, 22, 24

prairie — a large area of flat land that has tall grass and hardly any trees 13

predator — an animal that hunts other animals for food 13, 21

prey — an animal that is hunted by another animal for food 17

resident — a person or animal who lives in a particular place. You are a resident of your hometown 37

rodent — a kind of animal that has large front teeth for gnawing. Mice, rabbits, squirrels, and dormice are rodents 25, 33

salamander — an animal that looks like a small lizard. Salamanders do not have scales. Their skin is moist and soft 29

sow — mother pig 11

stag — adult male deer 35

stencil — a sheet of plastic or cardboard with a design cut into it used to draw specific shapes or patterns 6

tadpole — a baby frog or toad. Tadpoles live under water and have gills, a tail, and no legs 27